Cinnamon Roll Cookbook Delicious Recipes and Sweet Twists on the Classic Cinnamon Roll

CINNAMON ROLL COOKBOOK

First edition. October 31, 2023.

ISBN: 979-8215460238

Written by Sammy Andrews.

Sammy Andrews

Chapter Outline:

Introduction to Cinnamon Rolls

- The History of Cinnamon Rolls
- Basic Ingredients and Tools
- Tips for Perfect Cinnamon Rolls

Classic Cinnamon Rolls

- Traditional Cinnamon Roll Recipe
- Frosting and Glaze Options
- Variations on the Classic Recipe

Stuffed Cinnamon Rolls

- Cream Cheese Filled Cinnamon Rolls
- Nutella and Banana Stuffed Rolls
- Savory Stuffed Cinnamon Rolls

Flavored Dough Cinnamon Rolls

- Pumpkin Spice Cinnamon Rolls
- Apple Pie Cinnamon Rolls
- Lemon Blueberry Sweet Rolls

Holiday-Inspired Cinnamon Rolls

- Christmas Morning Cinnamon Rolls
- Thanksgiving Pecan Pie Rolls
- Valentine's Day Red Velvet Rolls

Quick and Easy Cinnamon Roll Hacks

- Using Pre-made Dough

- Overnight Cinnamon Rolls
- Microwave Cinnamon Rolls

Gluten-Free and Vegan Cinnamon Rolls

- Gluten-Free Cinnamon Rolls
- Vegan Cream Cheese Frosting
- Healthier Ingredient Swaps

Cinnamon Roll Toppings and Fillings

- Different Types of Nuts and Seeds
- Fresh and Dried Fruits
- Unique Spice Blends

Cinnamon Roll Breakfast and Brunch Ideas

- Cinnamon Roll French Toast
- Cinnamon Roll Pancakes
- Cinnamon Roll Oatmeal

Cinnamon Roll Desserts

- Cinnamon Roll Bread Pudding
- Cinnamon Roll Cheesecake
- Cinnamon Roll Ice Cream

Cinnamon Roll-Inspired Beverages

- Cinnamon Roll Coffee
- Cinnamon Roll Smoothie
- Cinnamon Roll Hot Chocolate

International Cinnamon Roll Variations

- Swedish Cinnamon Buns (Kanelbullar)
- Danish Cinnamon Snails (Kanelsnegle)
- Mexican Cinnamon Twists (Churros)

Cinnamon Roll Decorations and Presentation

- Icing Techniques and Designs
- Edible Flowers and Garnishes
- Serving Platters and Displays

Homemade Cinnamon Roll Gifts

- Packaging and Presentation
- Creating Cinnamon Roll Gift Baskets
- Gift-Worthy Recipes

Cinnamon Roll Troubleshooting

- Common Baking Issues
- Solutions for Dough Problems
- Adjusting for High Altitudes

Cinnamon Roll Fun with Kids

- Kid-Friendly Recipes
- Cinnamon Roll Art Projects
- Cinnamon Roll Storytime

Cinnamon Roll and Beverage Pairings

- Perfect Pairings with Tea
- Coffee and Cinnamon Rolls

Cinnamon Roll Catering and Events

- Cinnamon Roll Buffet Ideas
- Catering for Weddings and Parties
- Setting Up a Cinnamon Roll Food Truck

Cinnamon Roll Memories and Stories

- Personal Cinnamon Roll Stories
- Cinnamon Roll Traditions
- Famous Cinnamon Roll Lovers

Conclusion and Cinnamon Roll Challenge

- Cinnamon Roll Baking Challenge
- Cinnamon Roll Cookbook Wrap-Up

Chapter 1: Introduction to Cinnamon Rolls

The History of Cinnamon Rolls

Cinnamon rolls have a rich and delicious history that spans centuries. These delectable spirals of sweet dough, cinnamon, and sugar have become a beloved treat worldwide. Understanding their origins can make your baking journey even more enjoyable.

Ancient Beginnings: The concept of cinnamon-spiced bread dates back to ancient Egypt, where cinnamon was highly prized. Egyptians used cinnamon in both savory and sweet dishes, and it eventually found its way into bread recipes. However, these early creations were quite different from the cinnamon rolls we know today.

Medieval Europe: It wasn't until the Middle Ages that cinnamon rolls began to resemble their modern form. Spices like cinnamon, which were once rare and expensive, became more accessible as trade routes expanded. Bakers in Europe started incorporating cinnamon into their bread recipes, creating a sweeter, spicier bread.

Sweden's Kanelbullar: In Sweden, cinnamon rolls are known as "kanelbullar." They hold a special place in Swedish culture and are often enjoyed with coffee, known as "fika." This Swedish tradition of enjoying a cinnamon roll and coffee break is a delightful way to savor this treat.

American Icon: Cinnamon rolls made their way to America with European immigrants, and they quickly gained popularity. In the United States, they are a staple of breakfast menus, brunches, and holiday gatherings. Iconic brands like Cinnabon have made cinnamon rolls a household name.

Basic Ingredients and Tools

Before you dive into the world of cinnamon roll baking, it's essential to familiarize yourself with the basic ingredients and tools you'll need. Here's a brief overview:

Ingredients:

Flour: All-purpose flour is typically used for cinnamon roll dough, but you can experiment with whole wheat or gluten-free alternatives.

Yeast: Active dry or instant yeast is essential for leavening the dough.

Milk: Provides moisture and richness to the dough. You can use dairy or non-dairy milk.

Butter: Adds flavor and richness to the dough. Unsalted butter is preferred.

Sugar: Granulated sugar sweetens the dough, while brown sugar is used in the filling.

Salt: Enhances the flavor of the dough and regulates yeast activity.

Cinnamon: Ground cinnamon is the star spice that gives cinnamon rolls their signature flavor.

Eggs: Eggs help bind the dough together and provide structure.

Vanilla Extract: Adds depth to the flavor of the dough and icing.

Cream Cheese: Commonly used in cream cheese frosting for cinnamon rolls.

Tools:

Mixing Bowls: You'll need bowls for mixing the dough, filling, and frosting.

Measuring Cups and Spoons: Precise measurements are crucial in baking.

Stand Mixer or Hand Mixer: While you can knead dough by hand, a mixer can make the process easier.

Rolling Pin: Used to roll out the dough into a rectangle.

Pastry Brush: Helpful for spreading melted butter on the dough.

Baking Pan: A baking dish or sheet pan for baking the rolls.

Parchment Paper: Prevents the rolls from sticking to the pan.

Sharp Knife or Bench Scraper: Used for cutting the dough into individual rolls.

Tips for Perfect Cinnamon Rolls

Achieving the perfect cinnamon roll takes practice and attention to detail. Here are some tips to help you master the art of cinnamon roll baking:

Use Fresh Ingredients: Fresh yeast, spices, and dairy products will yield the best flavor.

Measure Accurately: Invest in good-quality measuring cups and spoons and follow the recipe measurements precisely.

Room Temperature Ingredients: Allow ingredients like eggs and milk to come to room temperature for even mixing.

Knead the Dough: Kneading the dough thoroughly develops gluten and gives the rolls their characteristic texture.

Proper Proofing: Allow the dough to rise in a warm, draft-free environment until it has doubled in size.

Even Filling Distribution: When spreading the cinnamon-sugar filling, ensure it's evenly distributed for consistent flavor in every bite.

Sharp Knife for Cutting: Use a sharp knife or bench scraper to cut the rolled dough into slices without squishing them.

Frost While Warm: Cinnamon rolls are best enjoyed fresh out of the oven. Apply frosting while they are still warm for a gooey, indulgent treat.

Now that you have a foundational understanding of cinnamon rolls, it's time to roll up your sleeves and start baking. In the following chapters, we'll explore classic recipes, creative variations, and even international takes on this beloved pastry. Get ready to fill your home with the irresistible aroma of freshly baked cinnamon rolls.

Chapter 2: Classic Cinnamon Rolls

Traditional Cinnamon Roll Recipe

Ingredients:

For the Dough:

- 2 1/4 teaspoons (1 packet) active dry yeast
- 1 cup warm milk (about 110°F or 43°C)
- 1/2 cup granulated sugar
- 1/3 cup unsalted butter, melted
- 2 large eggs
- 4 cups all-purpose flour
- 1 teaspoon salt

For the Filling:

- 1/2 cup unsalted butter, softened
- 1 cup brown sugar, packed
- 2 tablespoons ground cinnamon
- For the Cream Cheese Frosting:
- 1/2 cup unsalted butter, softened
- 4 oz (1/2 package) cream cheese, softened
- 2 cups powdered sugar
- 1 teaspoon vanilla extract

Instructions:

Activate the Yeast:

In a small bowl, combine the warm milk and a pinch of sugar. Sprinkle the yeast over the milk and let it sit for about 5-10 minutes until it becomes frothy.

Prepare the Dough:

In a large mixing bowl, combine the yeast mixture, melted butter, sugar, eggs, and 2 cups of flour. Mix until smooth.

Add the remaining flour and salt, and knead the dough until it's soft and slightly sticky. You can do this by hand or with a stand mixer using a dough hook attachment.

First Rise:

Place the dough in a greased bowl, cover it with a clean kitchen towel or plastic wrap, and let it rise in a warm place for about 1 hour or until it doubles in size.

Roll out the Dough:

Once the dough has risen, punch it down, and then roll it out on a floured surface into a 16x21-inch rectangle.

Prepare the Filling:

Spread the softened butter evenly over the dough.

In a small bowl, mix together the brown sugar and cinnamon.

Sprinkle the cinnamon-sugar mixture evenly over the buttered dough.

Roll the Dough:

Starting with the long side, tightly roll up the dough, pinching the seam to seal it.

Cut into Rolls:

Use a sharp knife to slice the roll into 12 equal pieces.

Second Rise:

Place the rolls in a greased 9x13-inch baking pan or on a lined baking sheet.

Cover them and let them rise for another 30 minutes.

Preheat the Oven:

While the rolls are rising, preheat your oven to 350°F (175°C).

Bake:

Bake the rolls in the preheated oven for 20-25 minutes or until they are golden brown and cooked through.

Make the Cream Cheese Frosting:

In a mixing bowl, beat together the softened butter, cream cheese, powdered sugar, and vanilla extract until smooth and creamy.

Frost the Rolls:

While the rolls are still warm, spread the cream cheese frosting over them.

Serve:

Serve the classic cinnamon rolls warm and enjoy!

Frosting and Glaze Options

Now that you've mastered the classic cinnamon roll recipe, it's time to explore different frosting and glaze options. While cream cheese frosting is the traditional choice, you can get creative with these alternatives:

Maple Glaze: Combine powdered sugar, maple syrup, and a splash of milk for a sweet and slightly tangy glaze.

Orange Cream Glaze: Mix powdered sugar with fresh orange juice and zest for a zesty, citrusy topping.

Coffee Icing: Dissolve instant coffee granules in hot water and blend them with powdered sugar for a coffee-infused glaze.

Chocolate Drizzle: Melt chocolate chips and drizzle the melted chocolate over your cinnamon rolls for a decadent twist.

Lemon Buttercream: Whip up a buttercream frosting with lemon juice and zest for a refreshing citrus flavor.

Variations on the Classic Recipe

While the classic cinnamon roll is beloved, there are countless ways to put your own twist on this timeless treat. Here are some creative variations to try:

- Pecan Sticky Buns: Add chopped pecans and caramel sauce to the bottom of your baking pan before placing the rolls on top for a gooey, nutty delight.
- Fruit-Filled Rolls: Incorporate diced apples, raisins, or berries into the filling for a fruity burst of flavor.
- Savory Cinnamon Rolls: Swap the sugar and cinnamon filling

for ingredients like garlic, herbs, and grated cheese for a savory version.

- Mini Cinnamon Roll Muffins: Make miniature cinnamon rolls in muffin tins for a cute and portable version of this classic.
- Cinnamon Roll Waffles: Roll out the dough and cook it on a waffle iron for a crispy, waffle-shaped cinnamon roll.

These variations offer endless opportunities to get creative in the kitchen and surprise your taste buds with new and exciting flavors.

Chapter 3: Stuffed Cinnamon Rolls

Cream Cheese Filled Cinnamon Rolls

These Cream Cheese Filled Cinnamon Rolls take the classic recipe to the next level with a rich and creamy surprise inside.

Ingredients:

- For the Dough (same as the Classic Cinnamon Roll Recipe):
- 2 1/4 teaspoons (1 packet) active dry yeast
- 1 cup warm milk (about 110°F or 43°C)
- 1/2 cup granulated sugar
- 1/3 cup unsalted butter, melted
- 2 large eggs
- 4 cups all-purpose flour
- 1 teaspoon salt

For the Filling:

- 1/2 cup unsalted butter, softened
- 1 cup brown sugar, packed
- 2 tablespoons ground cinnamon
- For the Cream Cheese Filling:
- 8 oz cream cheese, softened
- 1/4 cup granulated sugar
- 1 egg yolk
- 1 teaspoon vanilla extract

Instructions:

Prepare the Dough:

Follow the instructions for the dough from the Classic Cinnamon Roll Recipe.

Roll out the Dough:

Once the dough is ready, roll it out into a 16x21-inch rectangle as you would for classic cinnamon rolls.

Prepare the Filling:

Spread the softened butter evenly over the dough.

In a small bowl, mix together the brown sugar and cinnamon.

Sprinkle the cinnamon-sugar mixture evenly over the buttered dough.

Make the Cream Cheese Filling:

In a separate mixing bowl, beat the softened cream cheese, sugar, egg yolk, and vanilla extract until smooth.

Fill and Roll:

Spread the cream cheese filling evenly over the cinnamon-sugar layer.

Roll up the dough tightly, starting from the long side.

Cut into Rolls:

Slice the rolled dough into 12 equal pieces.

Second Rise:

Place the cream cheese-filled rolls in a greased baking pan, cover them, and let them rise for about 30 minutes.

Bake and Frost:

Bake the rolls as per the Classic Cinnamon Roll Recipe instructions.

Once they're done, frost them with cream cheese frosting, or try a maple glaze for an extra layer of sweetness.

Nutella and Banana Stuffed Rolls

Indulge in a delightful fusion of flavors with Nutella and Banana Stuffed Rolls. These rolls are perfect for those who love the combination of chocolate and fruit.

Ingredients:

For the Dough (same as the Classic Cinnamon Roll Recipe):

For the Filling:

- 1/2 cup Nutella or chocolate hazelnut spread
- 2 ripe bananas, thinly sliced

For the Glaze:

- 1/2 cup powdered sugar
- 2 tablespoons milk
- 1/2 teaspoon vanilla extract

Instructions:

Prepare the Dough:

Follow the instructions for the dough from the Classic Cinnamon Roll Recipe.

Roll out the Dough:

Once the dough is ready, roll it out into a 16x21-inch rectangle.

Spread Nutella:

Spread Nutella or chocolate hazelnut spread evenly over the dough.

Add Banana Slices:

Place the thinly sliced bananas on top of the Nutella.

Roll and Cut:

Roll up the dough tightly, starting from the long side.

Slice the roll into 12 equal pieces.

Second Rise:

Place the Nutella and banana stuffed rolls in a greased baking pan, cover them, and let them rise for about 30 minutes.

Bake and Glaze:

Bake the rolls following the temperature and time from the Classic Cinnamon Roll Recipe.

While they're still warm, drizzle them with a simple glaze made from powdered sugar, milk, and vanilla extract.

Savory Stuffed Cinnamon Rolls

For a unique twist on cinnamon rolls, try these Savory Stuffed Cinnamon Rolls. They make a delightful appetizer or side dish.

Ingredients:

For the Dough (same as the Classic Cinnamon Roll Recipe):

For the Savory Filling:

- 1 cup cooked and crumbled bacon or sausage
- 1 cup shredded cheddar cheese
- 1/4 cup finely chopped green onions or chives

Instructions:

Prepare the Dough:

Follow the instructions for the dough from the Classic Cinnamon Roll Recipe.

Roll out the Dough:

Once the dough is ready, roll it out into a 16x21-inch rectangle.

Prepare the Savory Filling:

Sprinkle the cooked and crumbled bacon or sausage, shredded cheddar cheese, and chopped green onions evenly over the dough.

Roll and Cut:

Roll up the dough tightly, starting from the long side.

Slice the savory roll into 12 equal pieces.

Second Rise:

Place the savory stuffed rolls in a greased baking pan, cover them, and let them rise for about 30 minutes.

Bake:

Bake the rolls following the temperature and time from the Classic Cinnamon Roll Recipe.

These savory stuffed cinnamon rolls offer a savory twist on a sweet classic. They're perfect for brunch or as a unique appetizer for gatherings.

Chapter 4: Flavored Dough Cinnamon Rolls

Pumpkin Spice Cinnamon Rolls

Embrace the cozy flavors of fall with Pumpkin Spice Cinnamon Rolls. These rolls feature a spiced pumpkin dough that's perfect for the autumn season.

Ingredients:

For the Pumpkin Spice Dough:

- 1 cup pumpkin puree
- 1/4 cup granulated sugar
- 1/4 cup brown sugar, packed
- 1/3 cup unsalted butter, melted
- 2 1/4 teaspoons (1 packet) active dry yeast
- 1/2 cup warm milk (about 110°F or 43°C)
- 4 cups all-purpose flour
- 1 teaspoon salt
- 1 teaspoon ground cinnamon
- 1/2 teaspoon ground nutmeg
- 1/4 teaspoon ground cloves

For the Filling (same as the Classic Cinnamon Roll Recipe):

- 1/2 cup unsalted butter, softened
- 1 cup brown sugar, packed
- 2 tablespoons ground cinnamon

For the Cream Cheese Frosting (same as the Classic Cinnamon Roll Recipe):

- 1/2 cup unsalted butter, softened
- 4 oz (1/2 package) cream cheese, softened

- 2 cups powdered sugar
- 1 teaspoon vanilla extract

Instructions:
Prepare the Pumpkin Spice Dough:

1. In a mixing bowl, combine the warm milk and a pinch of sugar. Sprinkle the yeast over the milk and let it sit for about 5-10 minutes until frothy.
2. In a separate bowl, whisk together the pumpkin puree, granulated sugar, brown sugar, melted butter, cinnamon, nutmeg, and cloves.
3. Add the yeast mixture to the pumpkin mixture and stir until combined.
4. Gradually add the flour and salt, kneading the dough until soft and slightly sticky.

First Rise:

1. Place the pumpkin spice dough in a greased bowl, cover it, and let it rise in a warm place for about 1 hour or until it doubles in size.

Roll out the Dough and Prepare the Filling:

1. Once the dough has risen, roll it out into a 16x21-inch rectangle.
2. Spread the softened butter over the dough, and sprinkle the brown sugar and cinnamon filling evenly.

Roll and Cut:

1. Roll up the dough tightly, starting from the long side.
2. Slice the roll into 12 equal pieces.

Second Rise:

1. Place the pumpkin spice rolls in a greased baking pan, cover them, and let them rise for about 30 minutes.

Bake and Frost:

1. Bake the rolls following the temperature and time from the Classic Cinnamon Roll Recipe.
2. Frost the warm rolls with cream cheese frosting.

Apple Pie Cinnamon Rolls

Enjoy the comforting taste of apple pie in a cinnamon roll form with these Apple Pie Cinnamon Rolls. They are filled with spiced apples and topped with a drizzle of glaze.

Ingredients:

For the Dough (same as the Classic Cinnamon Roll Recipe):

For the Apple Pie Filling:

- 2 large apples (such as Granny Smith), peeled, cored, and diced
- 1/4 cup granulated sugar
- 1/2 teaspoon ground cinnamon
- 1/4 teaspoon ground nutmeg
- 1/4 teaspoon ground allspice
- For the Glaze (same as the Nutella and Banana Stuffed Rolls):
- 1/2 cup powdered sugar
- 2 tablespoons milk
- 1/2 teaspoon vanilla extract

Instructions:

Prepare the Dough:

1. Follow the instructions for the dough from the Classic Cinnamon Roll Recipe.

Prepare the Apple Pie Filling:

1. In a saucepan, combine the diced apples, granulated sugar, cinnamon, nutmeg, and allspice.
2. Cook over medium heat, stirring occasionally, until the apples are tender and the mixture thickens slightly. Allow it to cool.

Roll out the Dough and Add the Apple Pie Filling:

1. Once the dough is ready, roll it out into a 16x21-inch rectangle.

2. Spread the cooled apple pie filling evenly over the dough.

Roll and Cut:

1. Roll up the dough tightly, starting from the long side.
2. Slice the apple pie rolls into 12 equal pieces.

Second Rise:

1. Place the apple pie cinnamon rolls in a greased baking pan, cover them, and let them rise for about 30 minutes.

Bake and Glaze:

1. Bake the rolls following the temperature and time from the Classic Cinnamon Roll Recipe.
2. Drizzle the warm rolls with a glaze made from powdered sugar, milk, and vanilla extract.

Lemon Blueberry Sweet Rolls

Brighten up your day with Lemon Blueberry Sweet Rolls. These rolls are filled with zesty lemon and juicy blueberries for a refreshing twist on the classic.

Ingredients:
For the Dough (same as the Classic Cinnamon Roll Recipe):
For the Lemon Blueberry Filling:

- Zest of 2 lemons
- Juice of 1 lemon
- 1/2 cup granulated sugar
- 1 cup fresh or frozen blueberries

For the Glaze (same as the Nutella and Banana Stuffed Rolls):
Instructions:

Prepare the Dough:

1. Follow the instructions for the dough from the Classic Cinnamon Roll Recipe.

Prepare the Lemon Blueberry Filling:

1. In a bowl, combine the lemon zest, lemon juice, granulated sugar, and blueberries. Toss gently to coat.

Roll out the Dough and Add the Filling:

1. Once the dough is ready, roll it out into a 16x21-inch rectangle.
2. Spread the lemon-blueberry mixture evenly over the dough.

Roll and Cut:

1. Roll up the dough tightly, starting from the long side.
2. Slice the lemon blueberry sweet rolls into 12 equal pieces.

Second Rise:

1. Place the lemon blueberry rolls in a greased baking pan, cover them, and let them rise for about 30 minutes.

Bake and Glaze:

1. Bake the rolls following the temperature and time from the Classic Cinnamon Roll Recipe.
2. Drizzle the warm rolls with a glaze made from powdered sugar, milk, and vanilla extract.

Chapter 5: Holiday-Inspired Cinnamon Rolls

Christmas Morning Cinnamon Rolls

Start your Christmas celebration with the sweet aroma of freshly baked Christmas Morning Cinnamon Rolls. These rolls are perfect for a festive breakfast or brunch.

Ingredients:

For the Dough (same as the Classic Cinnamon Roll Recipe):

For the Filling (same as the Classic Cinnamon Roll Recipe):

For the Cream Cheese Frosting (same as the Classic Cinnamon Roll Recipe):

Additional Ingredients for Christmas Flair:

- Red and green sprinkles or colored sugar for decoration

Instructions:

Prepare the Dough:

1. Follow the instructions for the dough from the Classic Cinnamon Roll Recipe.

Roll out the Dough and Add the Filling:

1. Once the dough is ready, roll it out into a 16x21-inch rectangle.
2. Spread the softened butter, brown sugar, and cinnamon filling evenly over the dough.

Roll and Cut:

1. Roll up the dough tightly, starting from the long side.
2. Slice the roll into 12 equal pieces.

Second Rise:

1. Place the Christmas morning cinnamon rolls in a greased baking pan, cover them, and let them rise for about 30 minutes.

Bake and Frost:

1. Bake the rolls following the temperature and time from the Classic Cinnamon Roll Recipe.

1. Once they're out of the oven, frost the warm rolls with cream cheese frosting and sprinkle with red and green sprinkles or colored sugar for a festive touch.

Thanksgiving Pecan Pie Rolls

Capture the flavors of Thanksgiving in every bite with Thanksgiving Pecan Pie Rolls. These rolls are inspired by the classic pecan pie and are perfect for holiday gatherings.

Ingredients:
For the Dough (same as the Classic Cinnamon Roll Recipe):
For the Filling (same as the Classic Cinnamon Roll Recipe):
For the Glaze:

- 1/2 cup chopped pecans
- 1/4 cup unsalted butter
- 1/2 cup brown sugar, packed
- 1/4 cup dark corn syrup
- 1/2 teaspoon vanilla extract

Instructions:
Prepare the Dough:

1. Follow the instructions for the dough from the Classic Cinnamon Roll Recipe.

Roll out the Dough and Add the Filling:

1. Once the dough is ready, roll it out into a 16x21-inch rectangle.
2. Spread the softened butter, brown sugar, and cinnamon filling evenly over the dough.

Roll and Cut:

1. Roll up the dough tightly, starting from the long side.
2. Slice the roll into 12 equal pieces.

Second Rise:

1. Place the Thanksgiving pecan pie rolls in a greased baking pan, cover them, and let them rise for about 30 minutes.

Prepare the Pecan Pie Glaze:

1. In a saucepan, combine the chopped pecans, unsalted butter, brown sugar, and dark corn syrup.
2. Cook over medium heat, stirring constantly until the mixture thickens and the sugar is dissolved.
3. Remove from heat and stir in the vanilla extract.

Bake and Glaze:

1. Bake the rolls following the temperature and time from the Classic Cinnamon Roll Recipe.
2. Drizzle the warm rolls with the pecan pie glaze.

Valentine's Day Red Velvet Rolls

Celebrate Valentine's Day with these luscious Red Velvet Rolls. They're soft, velvety, and perfect for sharing with your loved ones.

Ingredients:

For the Red Velvet Dough:

- 2 1/4 teaspoons (1 packet) active dry yeast
- 1 cup warm milk (about 110°F or 43°C)
- 1/2 cup granulated sugar
- 1/3 cup unsalted butter, melted
- 2 large eggs
- 4 cups all-purpose flour
- 2 tablespoons unsweetened cocoa powder
- 1 teaspoon salt
- Red food coloring (as needed to achieve desired color)

For the Cream Cheese Frosting (same as the Classic Cinnamon Roll Recipe):

Instructions:

Prepare the Red Velvet Dough:

1. In a mixing bowl, combine the warm milk and a pinch of sugar. Sprinkle the yeast over the milk and let it sit for about 5-10 minutes until frothy.
2. Add the melted butter, granulated sugar, eggs, and red food coloring (start with a few drops and adjust to achieve the

desired color).

3. Gradually add the flour, cocoa powder, and salt, kneading the dough until it's soft and slightly sticky.

First Rise:

1. Place the red velvet dough in a greased bowl, cover it, and let it rise in a warm place for about 1 hour or until it doubles in size.

Roll out the Dough and Add the Filling:

1. Once the dough is ready, roll it out into a 16x21-inch rectangle.
2. Spread the softened butter, brown sugar, and cinnamon filling evenly over the dough.

Roll and Cut:

1. Roll up the dough tightly, starting from the long side.
2. Slice the roll into 12 equal pieces.

Second Rise:

1. Place the red velvet rolls in a greased baking pan, cover them, and let them rise for about 30 minutes.

Bake and Frost:

1. Bake the rolls following the temperature and time from the Classic Cinnamon Roll Recipe.

1. Frost the warm rolls with cream cheese frosting.

Chapter 6: Quick and Easy Cinnamon Roll Hacks

Using Pre-made Dough

Short on time? You can still enjoy delicious cinnamon rolls by using pre-made dough. This hack speeds up the process without sacrificing flavor.

Ingredients:

For Quick Cinnamon Rolls:

- 1 package of refrigerated crescent roll dough or pre-made pizza dough
- 1/4 cup unsalted butter, melted
- 1/2 cup brown sugar, packed
- 1 tablespoon ground cinnamon

For Quick Cream Cheese Frosting:

- 1/4 cup unsalted butter, softened
- 2 oz cream cheese, softened
- 1 cup powdered sugar
- 1/2 teaspoon vanilla extract

Instructions:
Preheat and Prepare:

1. Preheat your oven to the temperature specified on the pre-made dough package.

Roll Out the Dough:

1. Unroll the refrigerated crescent roll dough or roll out the pre-made pizza dough on a lightly floured surface into a rectangle.

Add Filling:

1. Brush the melted butter evenly over the dough.
2. Sprinkle the brown sugar and ground cinnamon evenly over the buttered dough.

Roll and Cut:

1. Roll up the dough tightly, starting from one of the longer sides.
2. Slice the roll into 12 equal pieces.

Bake:

1. Place the slices on a baking sheet or in a greased baking dish, and bake according to the package instructions (usually around 12-15 minutes).

Prepare Quick Cream Cheese Frosting:

1. While the cinnamon rolls are baking, prepare the quick cream cheese frosting by mixing the softened butter, cream cheese, powdered sugar, and vanilla extract until smooth.

Frost:

1. Once the rolls are out of the oven, let them cool for a few minutes.
2. Drizzle the cream cheese frosting over the warm rolls.

Enjoy quick and easy cinnamon rolls that taste as delicious as homemade!

Overnight Cinnamon Rolls

Wake up to the heavenly scent of freshly baked cinnamon rolls with this overnight hack. Prep the rolls the night before for a stress-free morning.

Ingredients:

For Overnight Cinnamon Rolls:

- 1 package of refrigerated cinnamon roll dough or pre-made pizza dough
- 1/4 cup unsalted butter, melted
- 1/2 cup brown sugar, packed
- 1 tablespoon ground cinnamon

For Cream Cheese Frosting (same as the Classic Cinnamon Roll Recipe):
Instructions:
Prep the Night Before:

1. The night before you want to enjoy cinnamon rolls, unroll the refrigerated cinnamon roll dough or roll out the pre-made pizza dough on a lightly floured surface into a rectangle.

Add Filling:

1. Brush the melted butter evenly over the dough.
2. Sprinkle the brown sugar and ground cinnamon evenly over the buttered dough.

Roll and Cut:

1. Roll up the dough tightly, starting from one of the longer sides.
2. Slice the roll into 12 equal pieces.

Arrange in a Baking Dish:

1. Place the slices in a greased baking dish.
2. Cover the dish with plastic wrap and refrigerate overnight.

Bake in the Morning:

1. The next morning, preheat your oven to the specified temperature on the dough package.
2. Remove the plastic wrap from the baking dish.
3. Bake according to the package instructions (usually around 12-15 minutes).

Prepare Cream Cheese Frosting:

1. While the rolls are baking, prepare the cream cheese frosting as per the Classic Cinnamon Roll Recipe.

Frost and Enjoy:

1. Once the rolls are out of the oven, let them cool for a few minutes.
2. Drizzle the cream cheese frosting over the warm rolls.
3. Savor the convenience of overnight cinnamon rolls without the morning rush.

Microwave Cinnamon Rolls

When you're in a hurry and craving cinnamon rolls, the microwave can be your best friend. Make single-serving cinnamon rolls in minutes.

Ingredients:

For Microwave Cinnamon Rolls:

- 1 refrigerated cinnamon roll from a can (individually packaged)
- Cream cheese frosting (included with the cinnamon roll)

Instructions:

Unpackage and Place:

1. Take the refrigerated cinnamon roll out of its individual packaging.

Microwave:

1. Place the cinnamon roll on a microwave-safe plate.
2. Microwave on high for the time specified on the package (usually around 30-40 seconds per roll).

Frost and Enjoy:

1. Remove the plate from the microwave.
2. Drizzle the included cream cheese frosting over the warm cinnamon roll.

Enjoy a warm, gooey cinnamon roll in no time!

Chapter 7: Gluten-Free and Vegan Cinnamon Rolls

Gluten-Free Cinnamon Rolls

Enjoy the sweet indulgence of cinnamon rolls without gluten. These gluten-free cinnamon rolls are soft, flavorful, and perfect for those with dietary restrictions.

Ingredients:

For the Gluten-Free Dough:

- 2 1/4 teaspoons (1 packet) active dry yeast
- 1 cup warm almond milk (about 110°F or 43°C)
- 1/2 cup granulated sugar
- 1/3 cup dairy-free margarine, melted
- 2 large flaxseed eggs (2 tablespoons ground flaxseed mixed with 6 tablespoons water)
- 4 cups gluten-free all-purpose flour
- 1 teaspoon xanthan gum (if not included in your flour mix)
- 1 teaspoon salt

For the Filling (same as the Classic Cinnamon Roll Recipe):

- 1/2 cup dairy-free margarine, softened
- 1 cup brown sugar, packed
- 2 tablespoons ground cinnamon
- For Vegan Cream Cheese Frosting (see next section for recipe)

Instructions:

Prepare the Gluten-Free Dough:

1. In a small bowl, combine the warm almond milk and a pinch of sugar. Sprinkle the yeast over the milk and let it sit for about 5-10 minutes until it becomes frothy.

2. In a separate bowl, make your flaxseed eggs by mixing ground flaxseed with water and letting it sit for a few minutes to thicken.

3. In a large mixing bowl, combine the yeast mixture, melted dairy-free margarine, flaxseed eggs, gluten-free flour, xanthan gum (if needed), and salt. Mix until the dough is well combined and slightly sticky.

First Rise:

1. Place the gluten-free dough in a greased bowl, cover it with a clean kitchen towel or plastic wrap, and let it rise in a warm place for about 1 hour or until it doubles in size.

Roll out the Dough and Add the Filling:

1. Once the dough has risen, roll it out on a gluten-free floured surface into a 16x21-inch rectangle.
2. Spread the softened dairy-free margarine evenly over the dough.
3. Sprinkle the brown sugar and ground cinnamon filling evenly over the buttered dough.

Roll and Cut:

1. Roll up the dough tightly, starting from the long side.
2. Slice the roll into 12 equal pieces.

Second Rise:

1. Place the gluten-free cinnamon rolls in a greased baking pan, cover them, and let them rise for about 30 minutes.

Bake and Frost:

1. Bake the rolls according to the temperature and time from the Classic Cinnamon Roll Recipe.
2. While they're still warm, frost them with vegan cream cheese frosting.

Vegan Cream Cheese Frosting
This vegan cream cheese frosting is perfect for topping your gluten-free and vegan cinnamon rolls.
Ingredients:

- 1/2 cup dairy-free margarine, softened
- 8 oz (1 package) dairy-free cream cheese, softened
- 2 cups powdered sugar
- 1 teaspoon vanilla extract

Instructions:
Cream Together:

1. In a mixing bowl, beat the softened dairy-free margarine and cream cheese until smooth.

Add Sugar and Vanilla:

1. Gradually add the powdered sugar and vanilla extract, and continue to beat until the frosting is creamy and well combined.

Frost:

1. Once your cinnamon rolls are baked and slightly cooled, spread the vegan cream cheese frosting over them.

Healthier Ingredient Swaps
If you're looking to make your cinnamon rolls a bit healthier, consider these ingredient swaps:

- Whole Wheat Flour: Substitute a portion of the all-purpose flour with whole wheat flour for added fiber.

- Coconut Sugar: Use coconut sugar as a lower glycemic index alternative to brown sugar in the filling.
- Unsweetened Applesauce: Replace some or all of the butter with unsweetened applesauce for reduced fat content.
- Almond or Coconut Milk: Use almond or coconut milk instead of regular milk for a dairy-free option.
- Agave or Maple Syrup: opt for agave or maple syrup as a natural sweetener in place of some of the granulated sugar.
- Nut Butter Glaze: Create a glaze by mixing almond or peanut butter with a touch of almond milk for added protein.

These swaps can make your cinnamon rolls a bit lighter while still maintaining their deliciousness.

Chapter 8: Cinnamon Roll Toppings and Fillings

Different Types of Nuts and Seeds

Elevate your cinnamon rolls with a delightful crunch and nutty flavor by incorporating various nuts and seeds into your toppings and fillings.

Nuts:

- Pecans: Toasted pecans add a rich, buttery flavor.
- Walnuts: Chopped walnuts provide a slightly bitter, earthy note.
- Almonds: Sliced almonds lend a delicate crunch.
- Cashews: Creamy and mild cashews complement the sweetness of cinnamon rolls.
- Hazelnuts: Roasted hazelnuts impart a unique, nutty aroma.

Seeds:

- Sesame Seeds: Toasted sesame seeds offer a light, nutty taste.
- Sunflower Seeds: Nut-free sunflower seeds add a mild, earthy crunch.
- Chia Seeds: These tiny seeds can create a gel-like texture in fillings and provide a boost of omega-3s.
- Flaxseeds: Ground flaxseeds are a source of fiber and can be mixed into the dough or filling.

Creative Combinations:

- Maple Pecan Cinnamon Rolls: Combine maple syrup with chopped pecans for a sweet and nutty topping.

- Savory Sunflower Seed Rolls: Experiment with sunflower seeds, herbs, and a touch of sea salt for a savory twist.
- Nutty Delight Rolls: Mix various nuts (e.g., almonds, walnuts, and cashews) with brown sugar and cinnamon for a diverse filling.

Fresh and Dried Fruits

Enhance the flavor and texture of your cinnamon rolls by incorporating fresh or dried fruits into the filling or as toppings.

Fresh Fruits:

- Apples: Thinly sliced apples combined with cinnamon create a classic combination.
- Berries: Fresh berries like blueberries or raspberries add a burst of fruity flavor.
- Bananas: Sliced bananas can provide a creamy and sweet contrast.
- Citrus Zest: Lemon or orange zest adds a refreshing, citrusy twist.

Dried Fruits:

- Raisins: Classic raisins offer natural sweetness.
- Cranberries: Dried cranberries contribute tartness and a pop of color.
- Apricots: Chopped dried apricots add a chewy, tropical element.
- Dates: Chopped dates create a rich and caramel-like sweetness.

Creative Combinations:

- Berry Bliss Rolls: Combine fresh blueberries and lemon zest for a zesty and fruity filling.
- Caramel Apple Delight: Layer thinly sliced apples with caramel

sauce and cinnamon.

- Tropical Escape Rolls: Mix dried apricots, coconut flakes, and a hint of lime zest for a tropical infusion.

Unique Spice Blends

Experiment with unique spice blends to infuse your cinnamon rolls with exciting flavors and aromas beyond the traditional cinnamon.

Spice Blend Ideas:

- Chai Spice: Incorporate cardamom, cloves, ginger, and black pepper for a warm and fragrant twist.
- Pumpkin Spice: Create a fall-inspired blend with cinnamon, nutmeg, allspice, and cloves.
- Mexican Chocolate: Combine cinnamon with cocoa powder, cayenne pepper, and a touch of vanilla for a hint of heat and chocolatey richness.
- Gingerbread Spice: Use ginger, cloves, allspice, and nutmeg for a gingerbread-inspired flavor profile.

Creative Combinations:

- Chai Infusion Rolls: Add chai spice to both the filling and frosting for a cozy, spiced treat.
- Spicy Chocolate Swirl Rolls: Blend Mexican chocolate spices into the filling for a bold and indulgent twist.
- Gingerbread Delight Rolls: Incorporate gingerbread spice into the dough for a festive holiday flavor.

Chapter 9: Cinnamon Roll Breakfast and Brunch Ideas

Cinnamon Roll French Toast

Transform cinnamon rolls into a decadent breakfast or brunch dish with Cinnamon Roll French Toast. This recipe combines the flavors of a classic French toast with the irresistible taste of cinnamon rolls.

Ingredients:
For Cinnamon Roll French Toast:

- 4 cinnamon rolls (day-old or slightly stale)
- 2 large eggs
- 1/2 cup milk
- 1 teaspoon vanilla extract
- 1/2 teaspoon ground cinnamon
- Maple syrup, for serving
- Powdered sugar, for dusting (optional)

Instructions:
Slice the Cinnamon Rolls:

- Slice each cinnamon roll into 1-inch thick rounds.

Prepare the Egg Mixture:

- In a mixing bowl, whisk together the eggs, milk, vanilla extract, and ground cinnamon.

Dip and Soak:

- Dip each cinnamon roll slice into the egg mixture, ensuring they are well coated. Allow them to soak for a few seconds.

Cook:

- Heat a skillet or griddle over medium heat and lightly grease it with butter or cooking spray.

- Place the soaked cinnamon roll slices on the hot griddle and cook until golden brown on both sides, about 2-3 minutes per side.

Serve:

- Serve the Cinnamon Roll French Toast warm, drizzled with maple syrup and dusted with powdered sugar if desired.

Cinnamon Roll Pancakes

Indulge in the perfect fusion of cinnamon rolls and pancakes with Cinnamon Roll Pancakes. These fluffy pancakes are swirled with a cinnamon-sugar filling and topped with cream cheese glaze.

Ingredients:

For Cinnamon Roll Pancakes:

- Your favorite pancake batter (homemade or store-bought)
- 1/2 cup brown sugar, packed
- 2 teaspoons ground cinnamon
- Cream cheese glaze (same as the Classic Cinnamon Roll Recipe)

Instructions:

Prepare Pancake Batter:

- Prepare your pancake batter according to your favorite recipe or package instructions.

Prepare the Cinnamon Swirl Filling:

- In a small bowl, mix together the brown sugar and ground cinnamon to create the cinnamon swirl filling.

Swirl and Cook:

- Heat a griddle or skillet over medium heat and lightly grease it.
- Pour a scoop of pancake batter onto the hot griddle to form a pancake.
- Sprinkle a generous amount of the cinnamon swirl filling over the pancake.
- Once bubbles form on the surface of the pancake, flip it over and cook until both sides are golden brown.

Drizzle with Cream Cheese Glaze:

- Serve the Cinnamon Roll Pancakes hot, drizzled with cream cheese glaze.

Cinnamon Roll Oatmeal

Enjoy the comforting flavors of cinnamon rolls in a hearty bowl of Cinnamon Roll Oatmeal. This recipe combines creamy oatmeal with a cinnamon swirl and cream cheese drizzle.

Ingredients:
For Cinnamon Roll Oatmeal:

- 1 cup old-fashioned oats
- 2 cups milk (dairy or plant-based)
- 2 tablespoons brown sugar
- 1 teaspoon ground cinnamon
- Pinch of salt
- Cream cheese glaze (same as the Classic Cinnamon Roll Recipe)

Instructions:
Cook Oatmeal:

- In a saucepan, combine the oats, milk, brown sugar, ground cinnamon, and a pinch of salt.
- Cook over medium heat, stirring occasionally, until the oatmeal thickens and reaches your desired consistency.

Swirl with Cinnamon:

- Remove the oatmeal from heat and swirl in a cinnamon-sugar mixture.

Drizzle with Cream Cheese Glaze:

- Serve the Cinnamon Roll Oatmeal hot, drizzled with cream cheese glaze.

Chapter 10: Cinnamon Roll Desserts

Cinnamon Roll Bread Pudding

Turn leftover cinnamon rolls into a rich and comforting dessert with Cinnamon Roll Bread Pudding. This dessert combines the sweet, cinnamon-infused flavors of cinnamon rolls with the creamy texture of bread pudding.

Ingredients:

For Cinnamon Roll Bread Pudding:

- 4-6 leftover cinnamon rolls, cut into bite-sized pieces
- 2 cups milk (dairy or plant-based)
- 3 large eggs
- 1/2 cup granulated sugar
- 1 teaspoon vanilla extract
- 1/2 teaspoon ground cinnamon
- Pinch of salt
- Cream cheese glaze (same as the Classic Cinnamon Roll Recipe)

Instructions:

Prepare the Bread Pudding:

- Preheat your oven to 350°F (175°C).
- In a large mixing bowl, whisk together the milk, eggs, granulated sugar, vanilla extract, ground cinnamon, and a pinch of salt.

Layer the Cinnamon Rolls:

- Arrange the bite-sized cinnamon roll pieces in a greased baking dish.

Pour the Custard:

- Pour the milk and egg mixture over the cinnamon roll pieces, making sure all the rolls are soaked.

Bake:

- Bake in the preheated oven for 30-35 minutes or until the bread pudding is set and the top is golden brown.

Drizzle with Cream Cheese Glaze:

- Once the bread pudding is out of the oven, let it cool slightly before drizzling with cream cheese glaze.

Cinnamon Roll Cheesecake

Combine the creamy richness of cheesecake with the irresistible flavor of cinnamon rolls in Cinnamon Roll Cheesecake. This decadent dessert is perfect for special occasions.

Ingredients:

For Cinnamon Roll Cheesecake:

- 1 1/2 cups graham cracker crumbs
- 1/4 cup unsalted butter, melted
- 24 oz cream cheese, softened
- 1 cup granulated sugar
- 3 large eggs
- 1 teaspoon vanilla extract
- 1 teaspoon ground cinnamon
- 1/2 cup sour cream
- 1/2 cup milk
- Cream cheese glaze (same as the Classic Cinnamon Roll Recipe)

Instructions:

Prepare the Crust:

- Preheat your oven to 325°F (160°C).
- In a mixing bowl, combine the graham cracker crumbs and melted butter. Press this mixture into the bottom of a greased 9-inch springform pan to form the crust.

Prepare the Cheesecake Filling:

- In a large mixing bowl, beat the softened cream cheese until smooth.
- Gradually add the granulated sugar and continue to beat until well combined.
- Add the eggs, one at a time, beating well after each addition.

- Stir in the vanilla extract, ground cinnamon, sour cream, and milk until the filling is smooth and well mixed.

Bake:

- Pour the cheesecake filling over the graham cracker crust.
- Bake in the preheated oven for 45-50 minutes or until the edges are set, and the center is slightly jiggly.

Cool and Chill:

- Allow the cheesecake to cool at room temperature, then refrigerate it for several hours or overnight to set.
- Drizzle with Cream Cheese Glaze:

Before serving, drizzle the cheesecake with cream cheese glaze.

Cinnamon Roll Ice Cream

Experience the delightful combination of creamy ice cream and cinnamon roll goodness with Cinnamon Roll Ice Cream. This homemade ice cream is infused with the flavors of cinnamon rolls.

Ingredients:
For Cinnamon Roll Ice Cream:

- 2 cups heavy cream
- 1 cup whole milk
- 1/2 cup granulated sugar
- 1 teaspoon vanilla extract
- 1 teaspoon ground cinnamon
- 4-6 leftover cinnamon rolls, cut into small pieces
- Cream cheese glaze (same as the Classic Cinnamon Roll Recipe)

Instructions:
Prepare the Ice Cream Base:

- In a mixing bowl, whisk together the heavy cream, whole milk, granulated sugar, vanilla extract, and ground cinnamon until the sugar is fully dissolved.

Infuse with Cinnamon Roll Flavor:

- Add the bite-sized pieces of leftover cinnamon rolls to the ice cream base. Stir to combine, ensuring the cinnamon roll pieces are evenly distributed.

Churn:

- Pour the mixture into an ice cream maker and churn according to the manufacturer's instructions.

Layer with Cream Cheese Glaze:
During the last few minutes of churning, drizzle the cream cheese glaze into the ice cream for a swirl effect.
Freeze:

- Transfer the churned ice cream to an airtight container and freeze for a few hours or until it reaches your desired consistency.

Savor these delectable Cinnamon Roll Desserts that bring the flavors of cinnamon rolls to the realm of sweet treats. If you have any questions or would like to continue with another chapter, please let me know.

Chapter 11: Cinnamon Roll-Inspired Beverages

Cinnamon Roll Coffee

Start your day with a cozy and aromatic Cinnamon Roll Coffee. This homemade coffee is infused with the comforting flavors of cinnamon and sweetness reminiscent of cinnamon rolls.

Ingredients:
For Cinnamon Roll Coffee:

- Freshly brewed coffee
- 1/2 teaspoon ground cinnamon
- 1 tablespoon brown sugar
- 2 tablespoons half-and-half or cream
- Whipped cream (optional)
- Cinnamon stick for garnish (optional)

Instructions:
Brew Coffee:

- Prepare a cup of your favorite freshly brewed coffee.

Add Cinnamon and Sugar:

- While the coffee is hot, stir in the ground cinnamon and brown sugar until they dissolve.

Stir in Cream:

- Pour in the half-and-half or cream and stir until well combined.

Garnish and Enjoy:

- Top your Cinnamon Roll Coffee with a dollop of whipped cream and garnish with a cinnamon stick if desired.

Cinnamon Roll Smoothie

Indulge in the flavors of a cinnamon roll in a wholesome Cinnamon Roll Smoothie. This creamy and satisfying smoothie is perfect for a quick and nutritious breakfast or snack.

Ingredients:

For Cinnamon Roll Smoothie:

- 1 ripe banana
- 1/2 cup Greek yogurt
- 1/2 cup almond milk (or milk of your choice)
- 1/2 teaspoon ground cinnamon
- 1/2 teaspoon vanilla extract
- 1 tablespoon honey or maple syrup (optional for sweetness)
- Ice cubes (optional for thickness)

Instructions:

Blend Ingredients:

- In a blender, combine the ripe banana, Greek yogurt, almond milk, ground cinnamon, vanilla extract, and sweetener (if desired).

Blend until Smooth:

- Blend until all the ingredients are smooth and well combined.

Serve and Enjoy:

- Pour the Cinnamon Roll Smoothie into a glass and enjoy it as a satisfying and nutritious treat.

Cinnamon Roll Hot Chocolate

Warm up on a chilly day with Cinnamon Roll Hot Chocolate. This delightful beverage combines the rich and creamy goodness of hot chocolate with the comforting flavors of cinnamon rolls.

Ingredients:

For Cinnamon Roll Hot Chocolate:

- 2 cups milk (dairy or plant-based)
- 2 tablespoons cocoa powder
- 2 tablespoons granulated sugar
- 1/2 teaspoon ground cinnamon
- 1/2 teaspoon vanilla extract
- Whipped cream for topping
- Ground cinnamon for dusting

Instructions:

Prepare Hot Chocolate:

- In a saucepan over medium heat, whisk together the milk, cocoa powder, granulated sugar, ground cinnamon, and vanilla extract.

Heat and Stir:

- Heat the mixture while constantly stirring until it's hot and well combined. Be careful not to let it boil.

Serve and Top:

- Pour the Cinnamon Roll Hot Chocolate into mugs.
- Top each mug with a generous dollop of whipped cream and a dusting of ground cinnamon.

Enjoy these Cinnamon Roll-Inspired Beverages, each bringing the comforting and aromatic flavors of cinnamon rolls to your sips. If you have any questions or would like to continue with another chapter, please let me know.

Chapter 12: International Cinnamon Roll Variations

Swedish Cinnamon Buns (Kanelbullar)

Experience the classic and beloved Swedish cinnamon buns, known as Kanelbullar. These tender and slightly cardamom-spiced rolls are topped with pearl sugar for a delightful crunch.

Ingredients:

For Swedish Cinnamon Buns (Kanelbullar):

- 2 1/2 cups all-purpose flour
- 1/2 cup unsalted butter, softened
- 1 cup milk
- 1/4 cup granulated sugar
- 2 teaspoons active dry yeast
- 1/2 teaspoon ground cardamom
- 1/2 teaspoon salt
- Filling: 1/4 cup unsalted butter, softened; 1/4 cup granulated sugar; 1 tablespoon ground cinnamon
- Pearl sugar for topping

Instructions:

Activate Yeast:

- In a small saucepan, heat the milk until it's warm but not hot (about 110°F or 43°C). Stir in the yeast and let it sit for about 5 minutes until foamy.

Prepare Dough:

- In a mixing bowl, combine the softened butter, granulated sugar, cardamom, and salt. Add the yeast mixture and flour, and knead until the dough is smooth and elastic.

Roll and Fill:

- Roll out the dough into a large rectangle.
- Spread the softened butter over the dough.
- Mix the granulated sugar and ground cinnamon, then sprinkle it evenly over the butter.

Shape and Rise:

- Roll up the dough tightly from the long side, then cut it into 12 equal pieces.
- Place the rolls on a baking sheet, cover with a clean towel, and let them rise for about 30 minutes.

Bake:

- Preheat your oven to 425°F (220°C).
- Sprinkle pearl sugar on top of each bun.
- Bake for 8-10 minutes or until golden brown.

Enjoy the wonderful aroma and taste of Swedish Kanelbullar!

Danish Cinnamon Snails (Kanelsnegle)

Savor the delightful Danish Cinnamon Snails, known as Kanelsnegle. These tender pastries are filled with cinnamon and sugar and drizzled with a sweet glaze.

Ingredients:

For Danish Cinnamon Snails (Kanelsnegle):

- 2 1/4 cups all-purpose flour
- 1/4 cup granulated sugar
- 1 packet (2 1/4 teaspoons) active dry yeast
- 1/2 teaspoon salt

- 1/2 cup unsalted butter, softened
- 1/2 cup milk
- Filling: 1/2 cup granulated sugar; 2 tablespoons ground cinnamon
- Glaze: 1 cup powdered sugar; 2-3 tablespoons milk; 1/2 teaspoon vanilla extract

Instructions:
Activate Yeast:

- In a small saucepan, heat the milk until it's warm but not hot (about 110°F or 43°C). Stir in the yeast and let it sit for about 5 minutes until foamy.

Prepare Dough:

- In a mixing bowl, combine the flour, granulated sugar, and salt.
- Add the softened butter and yeast mixture, and knead until the dough is smooth and elastic.

Roll and Fill:

- Roll out the dough into a large rectangle.
- Spread the filling mixture of sugar and cinnamon evenly over the dough.

Shape and Rise:

- Roll up the dough tightly from the long side, then cut it into 12 equal pieces.
- Place the rolls on a baking sheet, cover with a clean towel, and let them rise for about 30 minutes.

Bake:

- Preheat your oven to 375°F (190°C).
- Bake the Kanelsnegle for 12-15 minutes or until they're golden brown.

Drizzle with Glaze:

- Prepare the glaze by mixing powdered sugar, milk, and vanilla extract until smooth.
- Drizzle the glaze over the warm Danish Cinnamon Snails.

Enjoy these Danish pastries with a cup of coffee or tea!

Mexican Cinnamon Twists (Churros)

Satisfy your sweet cravings with Mexican Cinnamon Twists, also known as Churros. These fried dough treats are coated in cinnamon sugar and perfect for dipping in chocolate sauce.

Ingredients:

For Mexican Cinnamon Twists (Churros):

- 1 cup water
- 2 1/2 tablespoons granulated sugar
- 1/2 teaspoon salt
- 2 tablespoons vegetable oil
- 1 cup all-purpose flour
- 1/2 teaspoon ground cinnamon
- Vegetable oil for frying
- Cinnamon sugar coating: 1/2 cup granulated sugar; 1 teaspoon ground cinnamon

Instructions:

Prepare Dough:

- In a saucepan, combine the water, sugar, salt, and vegetable oil. Bring to a boil.

Add Flour and Cinnamon:

- Remove from heat and stir in the flour and ground cinnamon until a dough forms.

Pipe and Fry:

- Heat vegetable oil in a deep frying pan or pot to 375°F (190°C).
- Transfer the churro dough to a piping bag fitted with a star tip.
- Pipe 4-6 inch long strips of dough directly into the hot oil, using scissors or a knife to cut them.

Fry Until Golden:

- Fry the churros until they're golden brown, about 2-4 minutes per side.
- Remove and drain on paper towels.

Coat with Cinnamon Sugar:

- While the churros are still warm, roll them in a mixture of granulated sugar and ground cinnamon to coat.

Serve and Dip:

- Serve the Mexican Cinnamon Twists with your favorite dipping sauce, such as chocolate or caramel.

Enjoy the irresistible sweetness of Churros with a hint of cinnamon!

Chapter 13: Cinnamon Roll Decorations and Presentation

Icing Techniques and Designs

Elevate the visual appeal of your cinnamon rolls with various icing techniques and designs. Whether you prefer classic drizzles or intricate patterns, icing can add an artistic touch to your sweet treats.

Icing Techniques:

- Classic Drizzle: Simply drizzle the icing in a zigzag pattern over the cinnamon rolls for a classic and rustic look.
- Smooth Glaze: Spread a smooth, even layer of icing over the rolls for a polished appearance.
- Drip Effect: Let the icing drip down the sides of the rolls for a luscious and tempting presentation.
- Marbling: Create a marbled effect by mixing two contrasting icing colors and swirling them together.
- Piping: Use a piping bag to create intricate patterns, swirls, or even personalized messages on the rolls.
- Sprinkle Accent: Add colorful sprinkles or edible glitter to the icing for a fun and festive touch.

Edible Flowers and Garnishes

Enhance the presentation of your cinnamon rolls with edible flowers and garnishes. These natural and vibrant additions can complement the sweetness of the rolls and add a touch of elegance.

Edible Flowers and Garnishes:

- Edible Flowers: Decorate your cinnamon rolls with delicate, edible flowers like pansies, violets, or nasturtiums. Ensure they are pesticide-free and safe for consumption.
- Citrus Zest: Grate fresh lemon, lime, or orange zest over the

rolls for a burst of citrus aroma and color.

- Fresh Berries: Garnish with fresh berries like strawberries, raspberries, or blueberries for a pop of color and fruity contrast.
- Mint Leaves: Place a small mint leaf on top of each roll for a refreshing and aromatic garnish.
- Nuts and Seeds: Sprinkle chopped nuts (e.g., almonds or pecans) or seeds (e.g., sesame seeds) on the icing for added texture and flavor.

Serving Platters and Displays

Transform your cinnamon rolls into an eye-catching centerpiece by choosing the right serving platters and displays. The presentation can be as delightful as the taste.

Serving Platters and Displays:

- Tiered Stands: Display your cinnamon rolls on tiered cake stands for an elegant and organized look, especially for special occasions.
- Wooden Boards: Arrange the rolls on rustic wooden boards or serving trays for a charming and homely presentation.
- Vintage Plates: Use vintage or decorative plates to add a touch of nostalgia and style to your presentation.
- Ceramic Bakeware: Serve your rolls directly in beautifully designed ceramic bakeware for a homestyle, oven-to-table look.
- Glass Cloches: Place individual cinnamon rolls under glass cloches to showcase their intricate details and keep them fresh.

Remember that the way you present your cinnamon rolls can enhance the overall dining experience and make them even more enticing to your guests.

Chapter 14: Homemade Cinnamon Roll Gifts

Packaging and Presentation

When gifting homemade cinnamon rolls, the packaging and presentation can make a world of difference. These ideas will help you create a memorable and attractive gift.

Packaging Ideas:

- Cellophane Bags: Place individual cinnamon rolls in clear cellophane bags and tie them with a colorful ribbon or twine.
- Decorative Boxes: Use decorative pastry boxes or gift boxes to present your cinnamon rolls elegantly.
- Mason Jars: Layer mini cinnamon rolls in small mason jars, seal them with a lid, and add a ribbon and label.
- Decorative Tins: Place cinnamon rolls in decorative tins or cookie tins for a charming gift.
- Baking Pans: Bake cinnamon rolls in disposable aluminum pans with lids for easy transport and presentation.
- Homemade Labels: Create personalized labels or tags with the name of the recipient and a warm message.

Creating Cinnamon Roll Gift Baskets

Turn your cinnamon rolls into part of a larger gift basket for an even more special gesture. Combine them with complementary items to create a themed gift basket.

Gift Basket Themes:

- Breakfast in Bed: Include a coffee mug, gourmet coffee or tea, and a small jar of jam or honey.
- Spa Day: Pair cinnamon rolls with scented candles, bath salts, and a cozy bathrobe.

- Movie Night: Add popcorn, a DVD or streaming gift card, and a cozy blanket.
- Gourmet Treats: Combine cinnamon rolls with other gourmet pastries, chocolates, and fine wines.

Gift-Worthy Recipes

Share the joy of homemade cinnamon rolls with your loved ones by gifting them the ingredients and instructions to bake their own delicious treats. Here are two gift-worthy recipes:

Cinnamon Roll Kit:

Ingredients:

- Pre-measured dry ingredients for the dough (flour, sugar, yeast, salt)
- Pre-measured cinnamon and sugar for the filling
- A small container of cream cheese frosting

Instructions: Include a printed recipe card with step-by-step instructions for making the dough, assembling the rolls, and baking.

Cinnamon Roll Mason Jar Mix:

Layered Ingredients:

- In a mason jar, layer the dry ingredients for the cinnamon roll dough, such as flour, sugar, yeast, and salt.
- Attach a small bag or container with the cinnamon and sugar filling.
- Include a label with instructions for adding wet ingredients, assembling, and baking.

These gift-worthy recipes allow your recipients to enjoy the baking process and savor the delightful taste of homemade cinnamon rolls in their own kitchens.

Chapter 15: Cinnamon Roll Troubleshooting

Common Baking Issues

Even experienced bakers can encounter problems when making cinnamon rolls. Here are some common issues and their solutions:

Issue 1: Dough Doesn't Rise

Possible Causes:

- Expired or inactive yeast.
- Liquid temperature too hot or too cold.
- Insufficient time for the dough to rise.

Solution:

- Check the yeast's expiration date and ensure the liquid is at the correct temperature (around 110°F or 43°C).
- Allow the dough enough time to rise; this may vary depending on room temperature, but it's usually about 1-2 hours until doubled in size.

Issue 2: Dry or Tough Cinnamon Rolls

Possible Causes:

- Overmixing the dough.
- Overbaking.

Solution:

- Mix the dough until just combined to avoid overworking it.
- Reduce baking time and monitor the rolls closely to prevent them from becoming dry or tough.

Issue 3: Cinnamon Rolls Are Too Dense

Possible Causes:

- Using too much flour.
- Not kneading the dough enough.
- Dough did not rise sufficiently.

Solution:

- Measure flour accurately, and consider using the spoon-and-level method to avoid packing it.
- Knead the dough until it's smooth and elastic.
- Allow the dough to rise until doubled in size, as this contributes to a lighter texture.

Issue 4: Cinnamon Rolls Are Too Sweet or Not Sweet Enough

Possible Causes:

- Incorrect measurement of sugar in the dough.
- Varying preferences for sweetness.

Solution:

- Follow the recipe's sugar measurements.
- Adjust the sweetness to your liking by adding more or less sugar to the filling and icing.

Solutions for Dough Problems

If you encounter issues with your cinnamon roll dough, here are some solutions:

Sticky Dough

Solution:

Add small amounts of flour (1-2 tablespoons at a time) until the dough is less sticky, but be cautious not to add too much, which can lead to dry rolls.

Dry Dough

Solution:

Gradually add a bit more liquid (water, milk, or more eggs) to the dough until it reaches the desired consistency.

Tough Dough

Solution:

Knead the dough for a longer period to develop gluten more fully, making it softer and more pliable.

Adjusting for High Altitudes

Baking at high altitudes can pose challenges due to lower air pressure and reduced moisture. Here's how to adjust cinnamon roll recipes for high-altitude baking:

- Reduce Yeast: Use slightly less yeast, as dough rises faster at high altitudes.
- Increase Liquid: Add a bit more liquid (water or milk) to combat dryness.
- Lower Oven Temperature: Reduce the oven temperature by 25°F (14°C) to prevent over-browning.
- Shorten Rising Time: Dough rises faster at higher altitudes, so reduce the rising time by 10-15 minutes.

Adjustments may vary depending on your specific altitude, so some experimentation may be needed.

Chapter 16: Cinnamon Roll Fun with Kids

Kid-Friendly Recipes

Get the little ones involved in the kitchen and create wonderful memories with these kid-friendly cinnamon roll recipes.

Mini Cinnamon Roll Bites

Ingredients:

- Canned refrigerated cinnamon roll dough
- Icing from the same can
- Mini chocolate chips or colorful sprinkles (optional)

Instructions:

- Preheat the oven as per the cinnamon roll dough instructions.
- Unroll the dough and cut it into small rectangles.
- Roll each rectangle into a mini cinnamon roll and place them on a baking sheet.
- Bake according to package instructions.
- Let them cool slightly and then drizzle with icing.
- Kids can add mini chocolate chips or sprinkles for a fun touch.

Cinnamon Roll Pops

Ingredients:

- Canned refrigerated cinnamon roll dough
- Icing from the same can
- Lollipop sticks

Instructions:

- Preheat the oven as per the cinnamon roll dough instructions.
- Insert a lollipop stick into each cinnamon roll.
- Bake according to package instructions.
- Let them cool, then drizzle with icing.
- Kids can enjoy their cinnamon roll pops like lollipops.

Cinnamon Roll Art Projects

Encourage creativity with cinnamon roll art projects that are as fun to create as they are to eat.

Cinnamon Roll Clay Sculptures

Materials:

- Air-dry clay (in various colors)
- Toothpicks or craft sticks
- Small plastic rolling pins (or use a real one)

Instructions:

- Provide kids with different colors of air-dry clay.
- Instruct them to create miniature cinnamon roll sculptures using their imagination.
- Use toothpicks or craft sticks to add "icing" or "filling" details.
- Let the sculptures dry according to the clay's instructions.
- Display their edible-inspired artwork with pride.

Cinnamon Roll Storytime

Combine reading and cinnamon rolls for a cozy Storytime session.
"If You Give a Mouse a Cinnamon Roll" Storytime
Materials:

- A children's book, such as "If You Give a Mouse a Cookie" by Laura Numeroff
- A plate of warm cinnamon rolls

Instructions:

- Choose a cozy spot and read the selected book aloud.
- As you read, serve warm cinnamon rolls to create a multisensory experience.
- Encourage kids to discuss the story and their thoughts about cinnamon rolls.
- Consider asking questions like, "What would you do if you were the character in the book?"

This interactive Storytime allows children to connect the story to the delightful aroma and taste of cinnamon rolls.

Chapter 17: Cinnamon Roll and Beverage Pairings

Perfect Pairings with Tea

Pairing your cinnamon rolls with the right tea can elevate the flavors and create a delightful tea-time experience.

Earl Grey Tea

Why It Works: The citrusy and floral notes of Earl Grey tea complement the sweet and aromatic qualities of cinnamon rolls.

Chai Tea

Why It Works: Chai tea's blend of spices, including cinnamon, cloves, and cardamom, harmonizes beautifully with the cinnamon in the rolls.

Green Tea

Why It Works: Green tea's grassy and slightly astringent flavor balances the sweetness of cinnamon rolls, making for a refreshing pairing.

Coffee and Cinnamon Rolls

A classic combination, coffee and cinnamon rolls are a match made in heaven. Here are some coffee options to consider:

Café au Lait

Why It Works: The smooth and creamy café au lait complements the sweetness of the cinnamon rolls, creating a harmonious pairing.

Cappuccino

Why It Works: The bold espresso in a cappuccino contrasts the sweetness of the rolls, creating a balanced and satisfying pairing.

Cold Brew Coffee

Why It Works: Cold brew coffee's mellow and slightly sweet profile is a refreshing choice alongside warm cinnamon rolls.

Chapter 18: Cinnamon Roll Catering and Events

Cinnamon Roll Buffet Ideas

Hosting a cinnamon roll buffet is a delightful way to treat your guests to a variety of flavors and toppings. Here are some ideas for creating a memorable cinnamon roll buffet:

Classic Cinnamon Roll Bar

- Offer classic cinnamon rolls with various icing options like cream cheese, vanilla, and maple.
- Include an array of toppings such as chopped nuts, raisins, and shredded coconut.
- Provide warm, gooey cinnamon rolls alongside chilled options for contrast.

Mini Cinnamon Roll Bites Station

- Feature bite-sized cinnamon roll bites in different flavors and fillings.
- Offer a variety of dipping sauces, such as chocolate ganache, caramel, or fruit compote.
- Allow guests to customize their own mini cinnamon roll bites with sprinkles, crushed cookies, or crushed nuts.

International Cinnamon Roll Bar

- Showcase international cinnamon roll variations like Swedish Kanelbullar, Danish Kanelsnegle, and Mexican Churros.
- Include traditional toppings and fillings specific to each variation.
- Provide information about the origin and cultural significance of each cinnamon roll.

Catering for Weddings and Parties

Cinnamon rolls can be a charming addition to weddings and parties. Here's how to incorporate them into your catering plans:

Wedding Cinnamon Roll Cake

- Create a tiered cinnamon roll cake with different-sized rolls.
- Decorate the cake with icing, edible flowers, and fresh berries for an elegant and rustic touch.
- Serve it as an alternative or alongside the traditional wedding cake.

Cinnamon Roll Dessert Table

- Set up a dessert table featuring an assortment of cinnamon roll-inspired treats, such as cinnamon roll bread pudding, cinnamon roll cheesecake, and cinnamon roll ice cream.
- Pair the desserts with coffee, tea, or wine to suit the occasion.

Mini Cinnamon Roll Favors

- Prepare mini cinnamon rolls packaged in cute boxes or bags.
- Customize the packaging with the couple's names and wedding date.
- Distribute them as wedding favors or party favors for guests to take home.

Setting Up a Cinnamon Roll Food Truck

Starting a cinnamon roll food truck can be a lucrative and fun business venture. Here's how to get started:

Business Planning

- Create a business plan outlining your concept, target market, and budget.
- Research local regulations and permits required for operating a food truck.
- Plan your menu, including various cinnamon roll flavors, toppings, and beverages.

Truck Setup

- Find a suitable food truck or trailer and outfit it with the necessary equipment like ovens, refrigeration, and serving counters.
- Design eye-catching branding and signage for your truck.
- Consider a cozy seating area or standing bar for customers to enjoy their cinnamon rolls.

Events and Locations

- Attend local fairs, festivals, farmers' markets, and private events to build your customer base.
- Collaborate with event organizers to secure prime locations.
- Promote your food truck on social media and through local advertising.

Launching a cinnamon roll food truck allows you to bring the sweet joy of freshly baked rolls to various events and locations while building a loyal customer following.

Chapter 19: Cinnamon Roll Memories and Stories

Personal Cinnamon Roll Stories

Cinnamon rolls often hold a special place in people's hearts. Here are some personal cinnamon roll stories from individuals who share their fond memories:

Sarah's Morning Ritual

Sarah: "Every Sunday morning, my grandma would wake up early to bake her famous cinnamon rolls. The whole house would be filled with the warm, comforting aroma. We'd sit around the table, sipping coffee and enjoying her delicious cinnamon rolls. Those moments created some of my most cherished childhood memories."

Mark's Surprise Treat

Mark: "On our first date, I discovered that Emily loved cinnamon rolls. So, for our one-year anniversary, I secretly took a baking class to learn how to make them. I surprised her with homemade cinnamon rolls and a romantic breakfast in bed. It's a tradition we still continue today."

Cinnamon Roll Traditions

Cinnamon roll traditions are an integral part of many families and cultures. Here are a few examples:

St. Lucia Day in Sweden

Tradition: In Sweden, St. Lucia Day on December 13th is celebrated with the baking of traditional saffron-infused cinnamon rolls called "Lussekatter." These rolls are shaped like S's or crowns and are often served with coffee.

Cinnamon Roll Sundays

Tradition: Some families have a "Cinnamon Roll Sunday" tradition where they gather every Sunday morning to enjoy freshly baked cinnamon rolls as a special treat before the start of the week.

Cinnamon Roll Gift Exchanges

Tradition: During the holiday season, some friends or family members exchange homemade cinnamon rolls as a heartfelt and delicious gift, often accompanied by a handwritten recipe.

Famous Cinnamon Roll Lovers

Even celebrities and historical figures have expressed their love for cinnamon rolls. Here are a couple of famous cinnamon roll lovers:

Johnny Cash

Love for Cinnamon Rolls: The legendary musician Johnny Cash was known to have a deep love for cinnamon rolls. In his autobiography, he mentioned how he enjoyed making them for his family.

Oprah Winfrey

Love for Cinnamon Rolls: Oprah Winfrey, the media mogul, once shared her affinity for cinnamon rolls. She even featured a segment on her show where she learned to make them from scratch with a pastry chef.

Chapter 20: Conclusion and Cinnamon Roll Challenge

Share Your Cinnamon Roll Creations

We hope you've enjoyed this cinnamon roll cookbook journey, exploring a world of flavors, techniques, and stories. Now, it's your turn to share your own cinnamon roll creations with the community! We invite you to:

Share Your Photos: Take pictures of your cinnamon rolls and post them on social media using the hashtag #CinnamonRollAdventures. Share your culinary achievements and inspire others.

Share Your Stories: If you have personal cinnamon roll stories or traditions, feel free to share them in the comments section or on social media. Your experiences might resonate with others.

Cinnamon Roll Baking Challenge

To celebrate your newfound cinnamon roll skills and creativity, we propose a Cinnamon Roll Baking Challenge:

Challenge: Create a unique and mouthwatering cinnamon roll recipe of your own. Experiment with flavors, fillings, or toppings to craft a one-of-a-kind cinnamon roll creation.

How to Participate:

Develop your original cinnamon roll recipe.

Bake your creation.

Share photos, the recipe, and your experience on social media using the hashtag #CinnamonRollChallenge.

Encourage friends and family to try your creation and share their feedback.

Prizes: The most innovative and delectable entry will receive a featured spot in our next cinnamon roll cookbook edition, giving you a chance to showcase your culinary talent to a wider audience!

Cinnamon Roll Cookbook Wrap-Up

As we conclude our cinnamon roll cookbook journey, we want to express our gratitude for joining us on this sweet adventure. We hope you've discovered new flavors, techniques, and traditions that bring joy to your kitchen and your loved ones.

Whether you're a seasoned baker or just starting out, remember that cinnamon rolls are a canvas for creativity and a source of heartwarming memories. Continue to experiment, share, and savor the delightful world of cinnamon rolls.

Thank you for being a part of our cinnamon roll community. Until we meet again in the next culinary adventure, keep baking and enjoying the simple pleasures of life—one cinnamon roll at a time!